who is she when she is not her

The Open Gates Of Thoughts

PARI JOG

ISBN 979-8-89066-834-9

Contents

Waves

They said happiness comes in waves,

It'll find you again.

But you came rushing in like a storm,

And before I knew it, I was drowning in a beautiful disaster.

Twin Stars

Can you hear my heart?

Oh, but can I tell!

We are twin stars

With different births.

My caring shadow–

It has your face.

The voice of my soul,

Knows well your name.

Strange Time

Time is a strange story

And a lonely story of people,

Of past and nothingness

Time is a strange story of miracle.

Where the planets exist in thousand galaxies

Our life is a strange story,

Where wounds go deep uprooted roots

And flowers are still alive at midnight.

Birthdays

What they don't understand about birthdays and what they never tell you is that when you're eleven,

You're also ten, nine, eight, seven, six, five, four, three, two, one.

And when you wake up on your eleventh birthday,

You expect to feel eleven but you don't.

You open your eyes and everything's just like yesterday.

She

She lost herself in the trees, among the ever-changing leaves. She wept beneath the wild sky as stars told stories of ancient times.

Time flowers grew towards her light,

The river called her name at night.

She could not live an ordinary life with the mysteries of the universe hidden in her eyes.

Dreams

The worst thing that you believe is that your happiest lies within someone else; you never put your happiness in the fragile hands of others.

You put in your goals,

Your achievements,

You put your happiness in your passion…

In the things that matter because people will never reward you like your dreams will.

Trauma Changes Us

This is the big, scary truth about trauma,

There is no such thing as "getting over it."

The five stages of grief modal mark

Universal stages in learning to accept loss,

But the reality is in fact much bigger:

A major life disruption leaves a new normal in its wake.
There is no "back to the old me."

You are different now, full stop.

This is not a wholly negative thing,

Healing from trauma can also mean finalising new strength
and joy.

The goal of healing is not a papering-over of changes in an
effort to preserve or present things as normal.

It is to acknowledge and wear your new life wars, wisdom,
and all with courage.

Trauma Steals Your Voice

People get so tired of asking what's wrong and you've run out of nothing to tell them,

You've tried and they've tried,

But the words just turn to ashes every time they try to leave your mouth.

Background

I am the girl

No one looked twice at.

I am not popular,

I am unknown,

I don't have 2 million friends

I have 2,

I am pretty but not

gorgeous,

Im likeable not loveable.

And Im the background character

Not the main one.

I was a fool to think you thought different.

"waiting for you in the background was my mistake."

Remember

When every dream has turned into dust,

And your highest hopes no longer soar.

When places you once yearned to see,

Grow further away on distant shores.

When every night you close your eyes,

And don't long inside for something more.

Remember this and only this,

If nothing else you recall.

There was a life,

A girl lived once,

Where you were loved the most of all.

Who Am I?

Who am I?

Who am I really,

When all the layers of others' opinions,

Expectations, and definition

Are peeled away?

Who am I beneath all the layers

Society, friends, and family

Have wrapped me tightly into

Like a straitjacket almost impossible to escape?

Who am I,

When I look at myself in the mirror

And see me with clear eyes

Without the filters of others?

That's what I'm trying to find out

That's what I'm trying to see…

It's a journey

Without a clear finish line.

Pretty Is a Lie

What if I told you, the word "pretty" is a skin

Deep, six-letter prison they put you in.

They say, "If you lost some weight, you'd be so pretty."

They say, "If your skin was clearer, you'd be so pretty."

But what they really mean is, "If only you looked like our mass-produced ideal, you'd be so pretty."

Let me tell you a secret they do not want you to know, nothing about you is pretty nor will it ever be so.

You see, pretty is too small and simple a word to capture the exquisitely complex human phenomenon you are, every atom of you was plucked in the quiet cosmic moments between supernovas and stars,

A carefully chosen palette of your skin, your eyes,

Your muscles and bones from sunsets and skies.

So when they tell you about how pretty you could be if only.

Cut them off and say "pretty" is not your worth or value or something you have ever aspired to be.

If You Could See It

If you could see your soul tonight,

How much would you grieve

For the damage

It has suffered

At the hands of those

Who treated it so cruelly?

Poem

I will never be a poem,

Beautifully written and composed.

I will never be a song,

Remembered and euphonious.

I will never be a novel,

Coherent and captivating.

I will forever be the unwritten thought,

The half-finished story,

The long-forgotten melody.

Star

They witnessed her destruction,

Then were left to wonder why,

She saw nothing but darkness,

Though the stars shone in her eyes.

But maybe they'd forgotten,

When they failed to see the cracks,

That a star's light shines the brightest,

When it's starting to collapse.

Warrior

And that was the thing about her,

She kept on surviving.

With bullet holes in her lungs,

And knife marks etched on her back.

She never let anything in her way,

Resilient.

A fighter,

Not by choice

But a warrior at heart.

Changed

She's changed.

You can see it in her eyes,

Feel it in her touch,

Hear it in her tone.

She's not the same.

And she's never coming back.

Moon

And like the moon,

She had a side of her

So dark, that even the stars

Couldn't shine on it;

She had a side of her

So cold, that even the sun

Couldn't burn on it.

Mama

Mama, I hope you're proud of me.

I took all the awful things they did,

And turned them into empathy.

Mama, I hope you're proud of me,

I may have let their poison under my skin,

But I let it drip out of my fingers as poetry.

Ashes

Before she became fire, she was water.

Enjoying the thunderstorm

She gave and she gave

She never looked at what she had

Until she turned from sea to desert.

But instead of dying of the heat, the warm,

the sadness, the heartache,

She took all of her pain

And from her own ashes became fire.

Fire that did not have anything of its own

Fire that gave light to everyone.

She was incandescently beautiful

And beauty was the least of her.

She didn't want love,

She wanted to be loved.

And that

Was entirely different.

Pain

Pain, she was the kind of girl who talks about pain with so much ignorance.

Ignorance of hate and acceptance of love and lesson.

She was the kind of girl who sees the pain of others with much passion.

The pain that caused her heart to bleed too.

She was the kind of girl who would use her red blood too paint the world with bliss.

She is the kind of girl who carries her beauty in her eyes and I guess

That's all that she needed to make a difference.

www.ingramcontent.com/pod-product-compliance
Lightning Source LLC
Chambersburg PA
CBHW022122150726
47990CB00003B/1462